These works are a tribute to the American Artist, Lee Bontecou. I came across her sculptural works of steel and fabric about twenty years ago, and was mesmerized by them. Something about the ominous presence of these holes, the dark nature of them, the 'Space Age' feeling, almost like jet engines.

Over the past few decades, I had began making works based on this idea of fabric stretched and stiched over a steel frame. The first works, a set of fish. However, in 2021 I began making more direct works around them. As her pieces seemed to have a language of parts, a hole, a vent, a rib, I created my own language about them, and after making a few different works with this language, I began creating this series.

The result are these pieces: A tribute, in a language I evolved from the original works, but based around my interpretation of their strongest aspects.

I hope you enjoy them!

-Gary

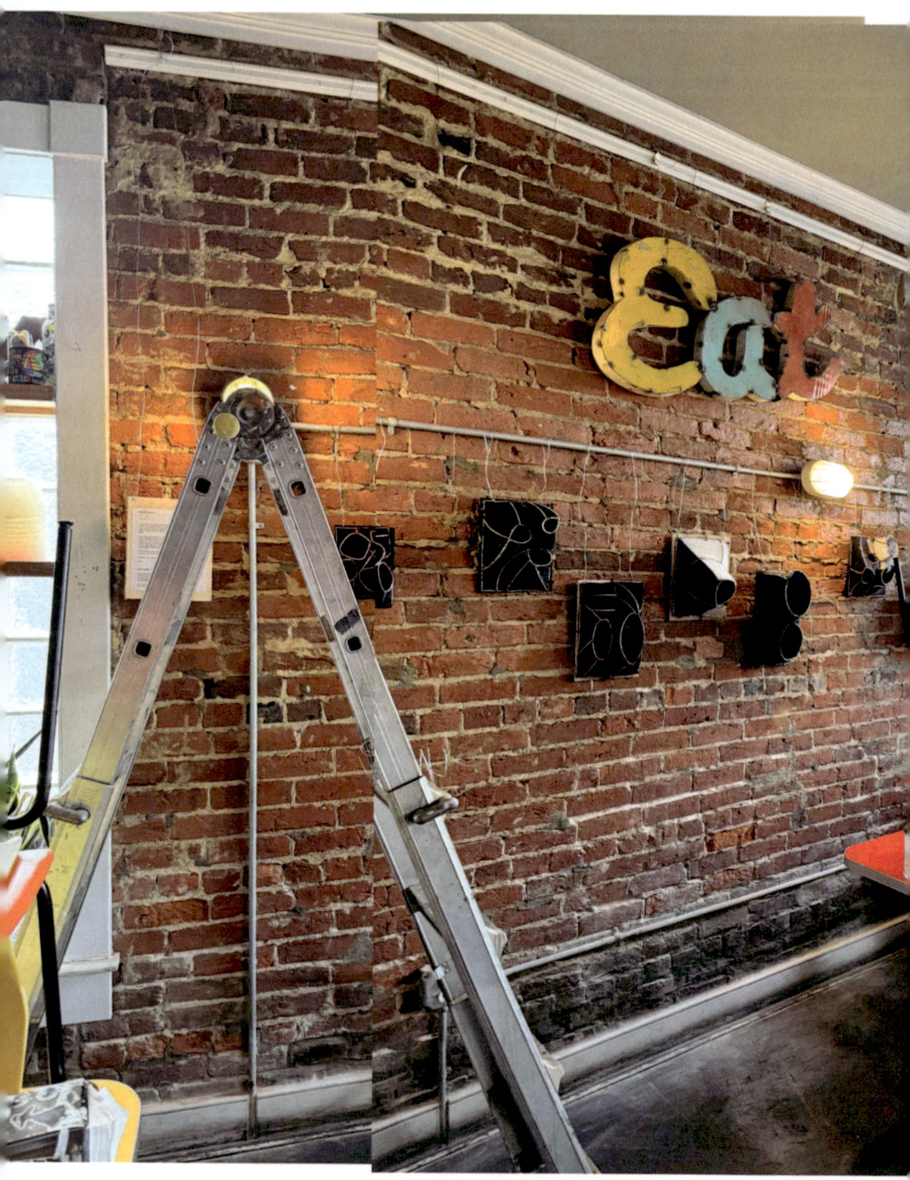

eat

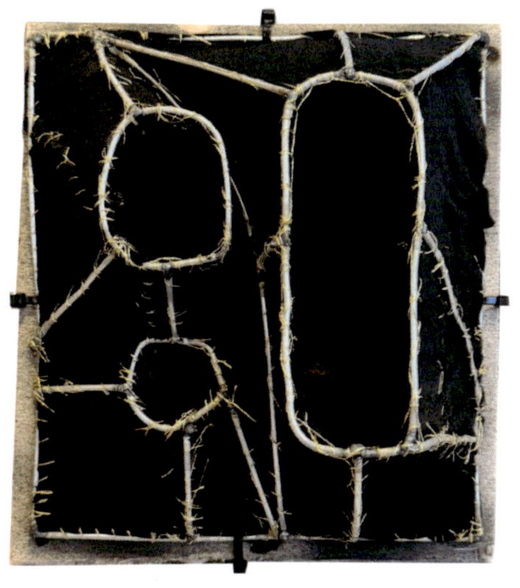

'Bontecaux #10'
Welded steel wire, cotton fabric,
thread, zip ties, on wood panel
8x9x4.5"
2024

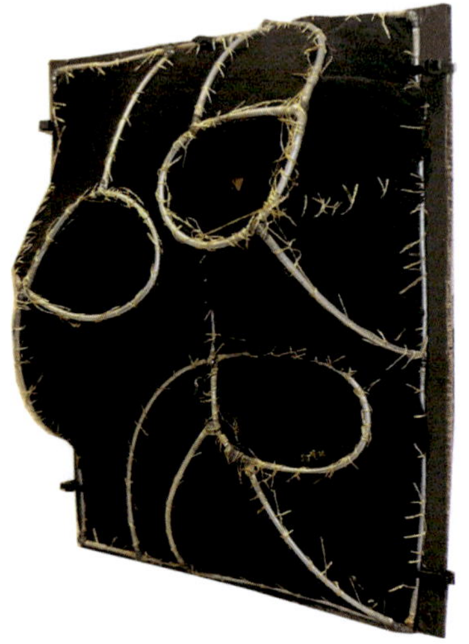

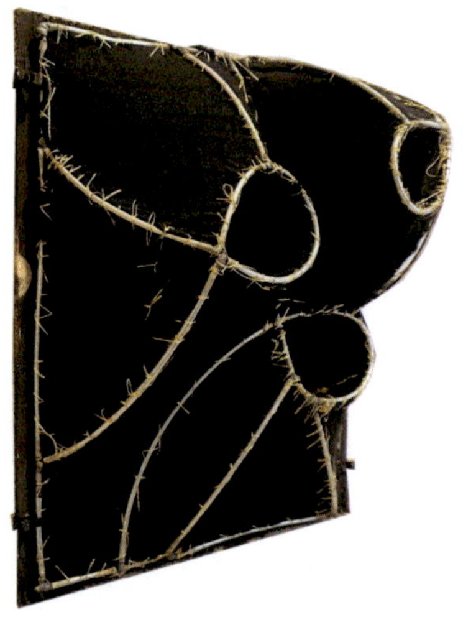

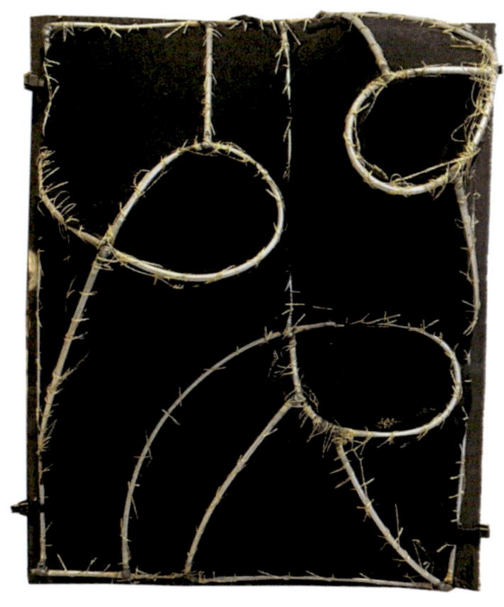

'Bontecaux #9'
Welded steel wire, cotton fabric,
thread, zip ties, on wood panel
10x8x4"
2024

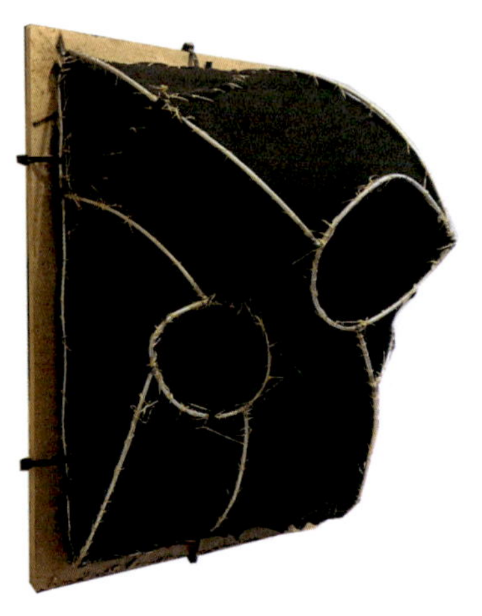

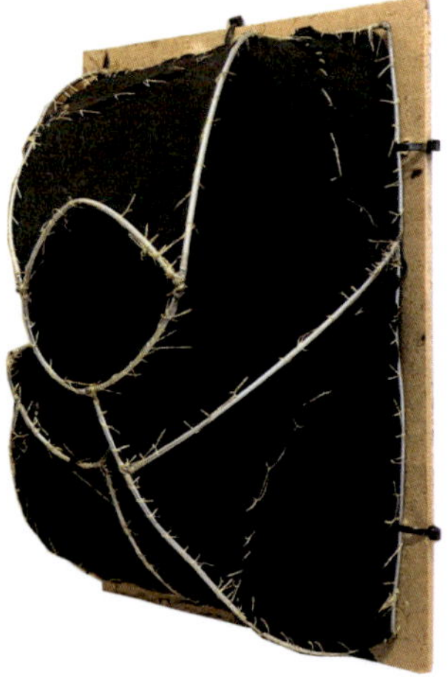

Library of Congress Control Number:
2024950993

ISBN: 979-8-9909185-6-6

OVOLR! / Debackle
Richmond, VA

'BONTECAUX's

GARY LLAMA

OVOLR! / DEBACKLE
RICHMOND, VIRGINIA

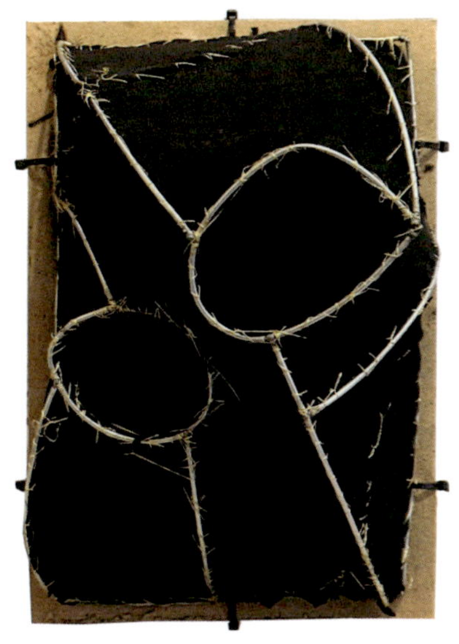

'Bontecaux #8'
Welded steel wire, canvas, thread, zip
ties, on wood panel
9x13x6"
2024

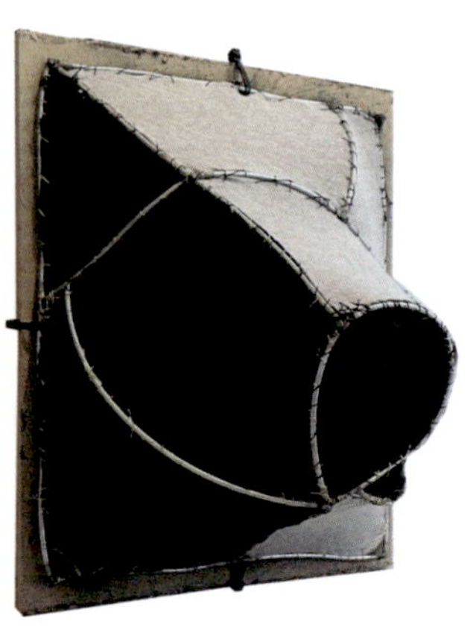

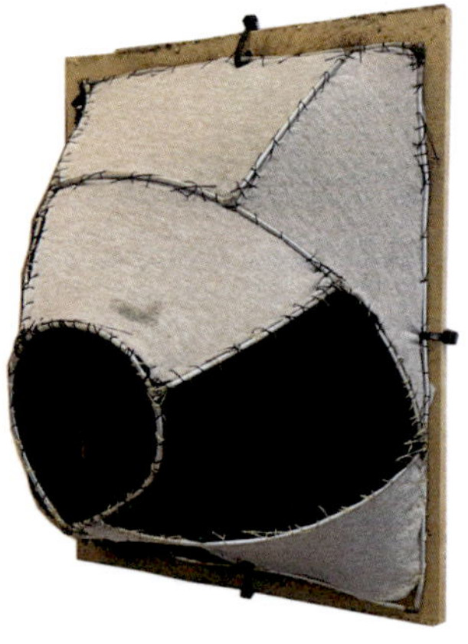

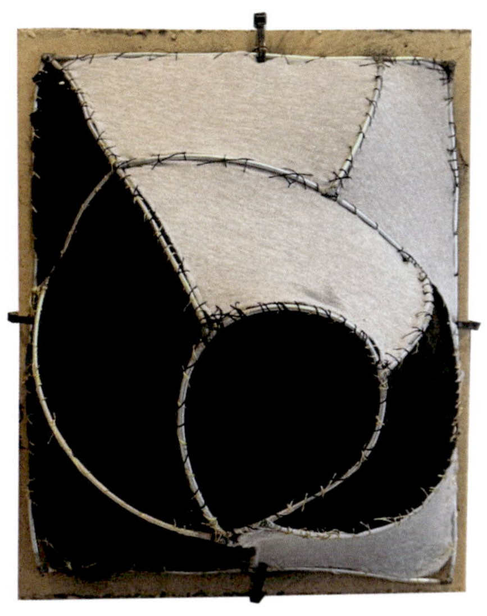

'Bontecaux #7'
Welded steel wire, canvas, thread, zip
ties, on wood panel
11x9x6"
2024

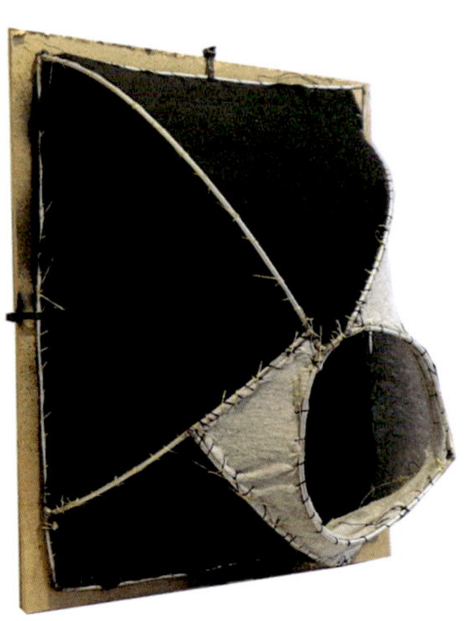

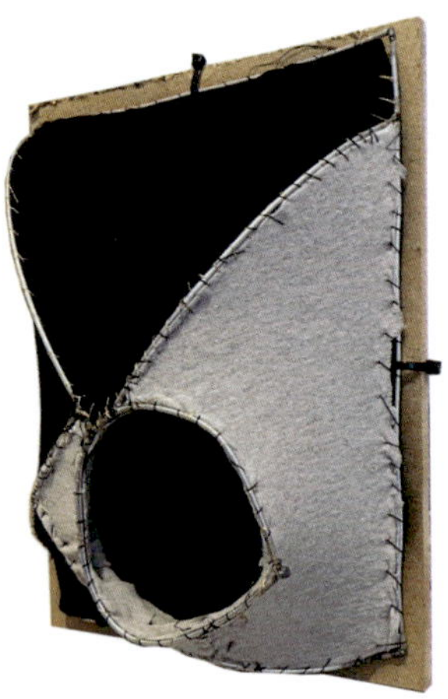

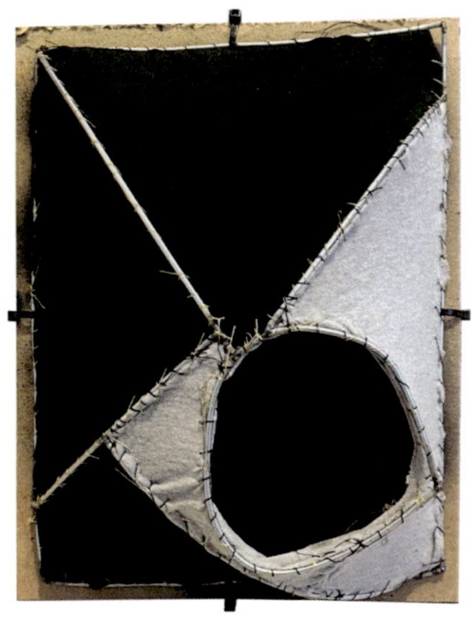

'Bontecaux #6'
Welded steel wire, canvas, thread, zip
ties, on wood panel
11.5x9x4.5"
2024

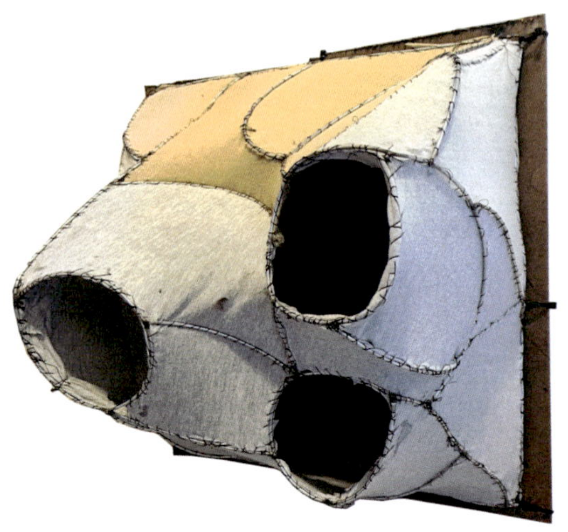

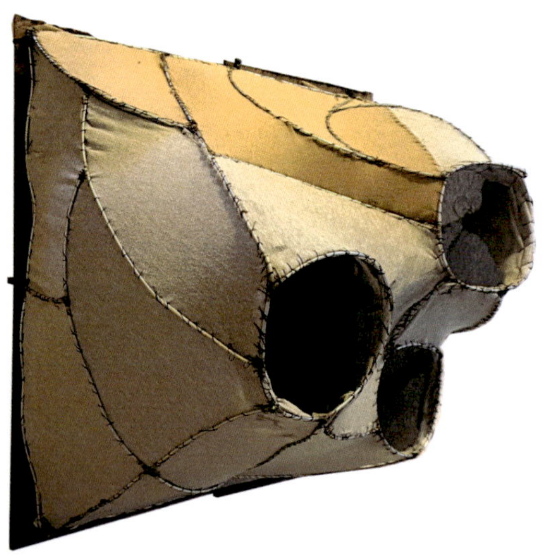

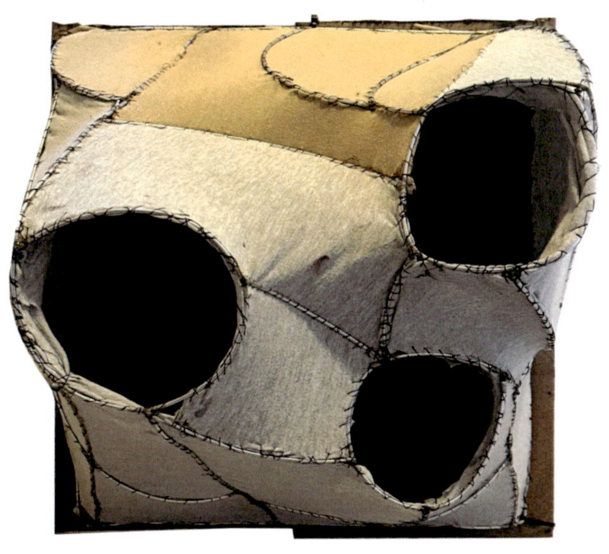

'Bontecaux #5'
Welded steel wire, canvas, thread, zip
ties, on wood panel
17.5x17.5x10.5"
2024

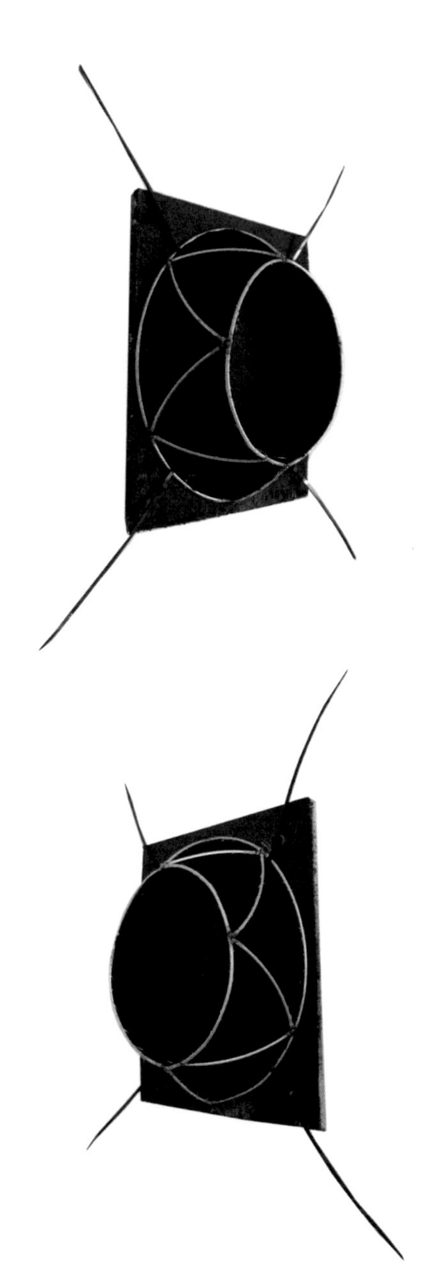

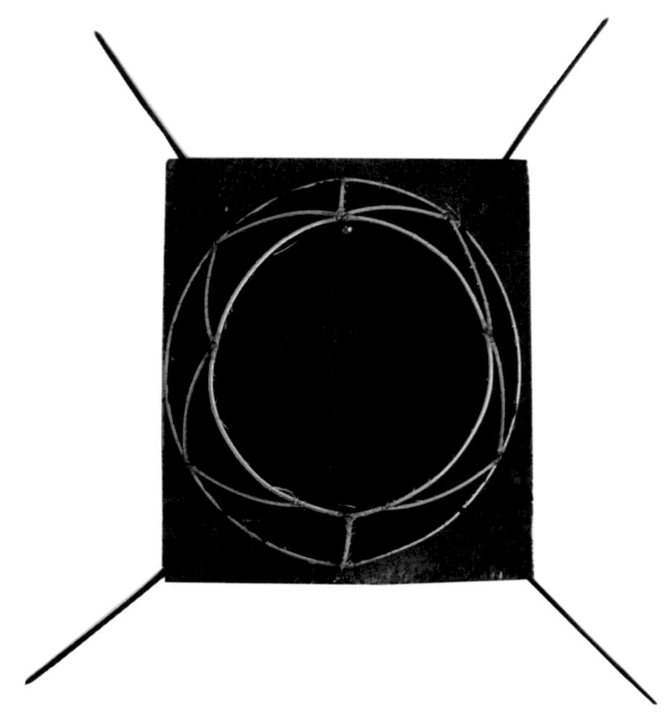

'Bontecaux #4'
Welded steel wire, canvas, thread, zip
ties, on wood panel
20x20x2.5"
2023

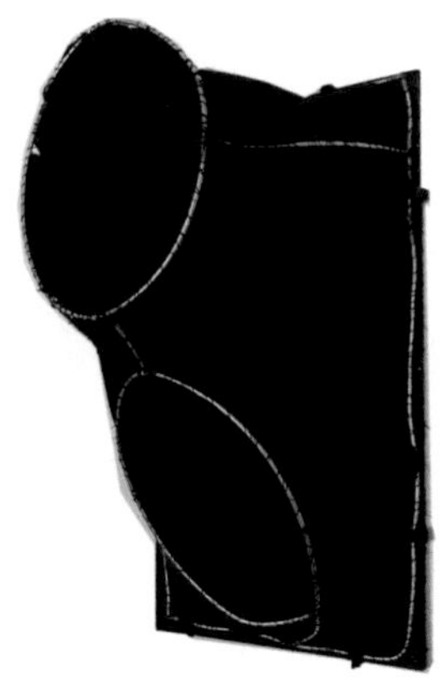

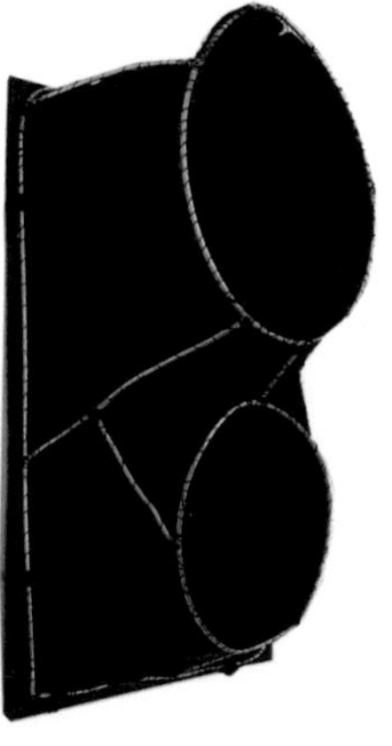

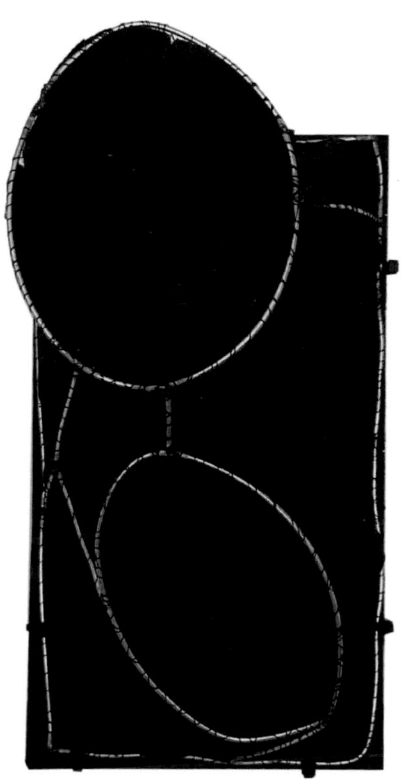

'Bontecaux #3'
Welded steel wire, canvas, thread, zip
ties, on wood panel
13.75x7.5x8"
2023

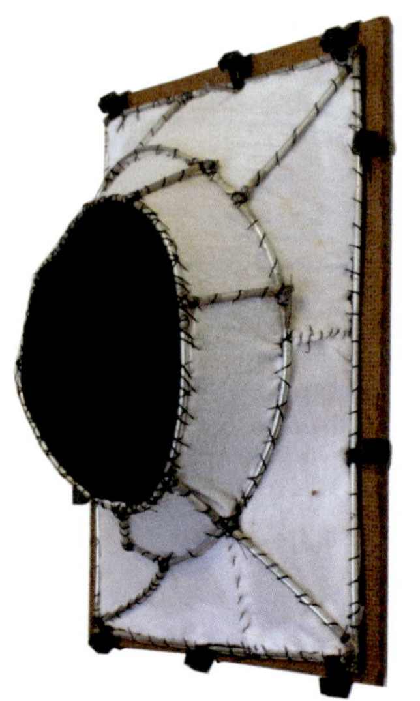

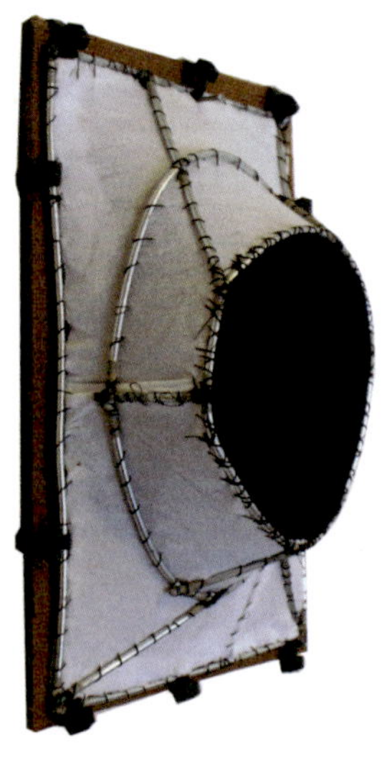

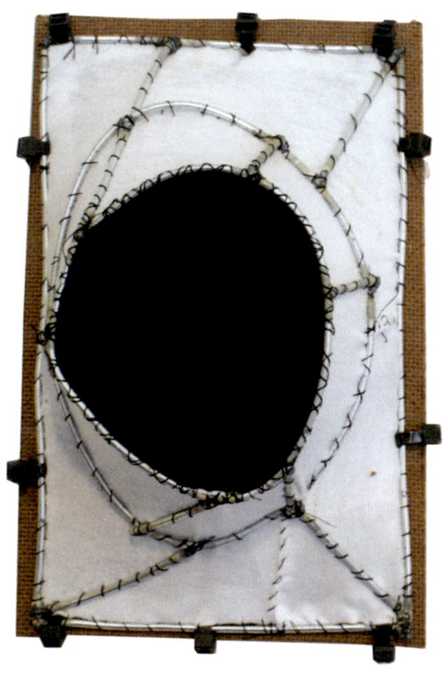

'Bontecaux (mini)'
Wire, fabric, thread, solder
3x4x1"
2021

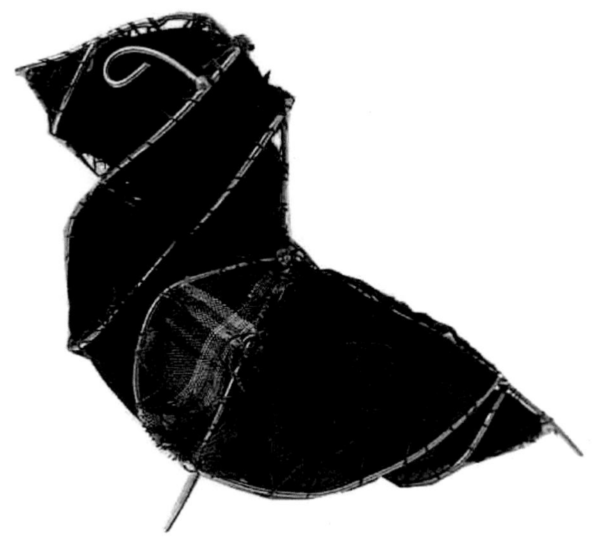

'Bontecaux (bird)'
Wire, fabric, thread, solder
3x4x1.5"
2021

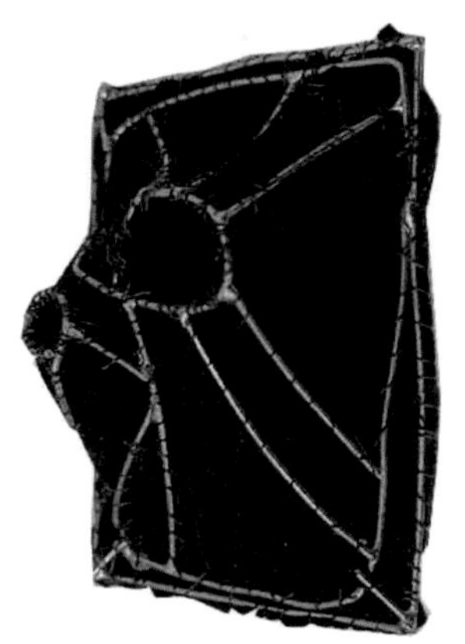

'Bontecaux (miniature)'
Welded steel wire, cotton, zip ties, on
wood panel
8.5x5.75x3"
2023

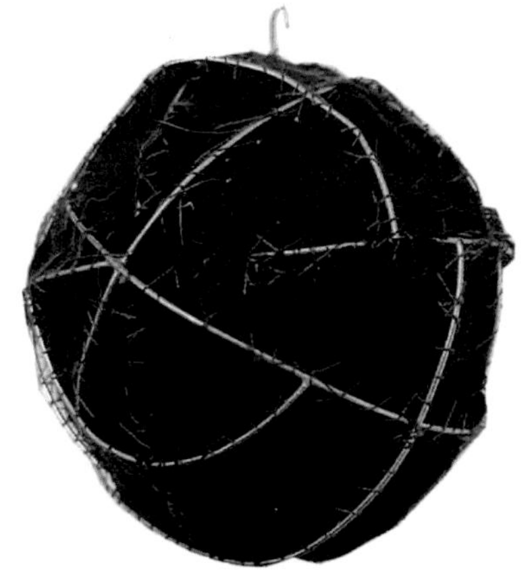

'Bontecaux (ball)'
Wire, fabric, thread, solder
5" round (approx.)
2021

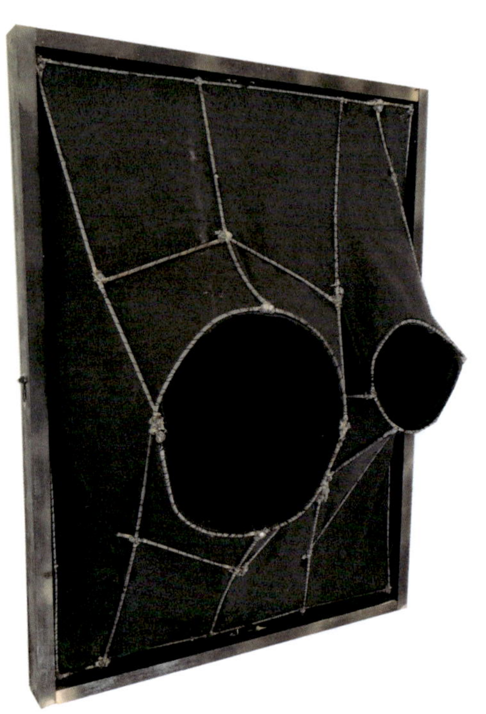

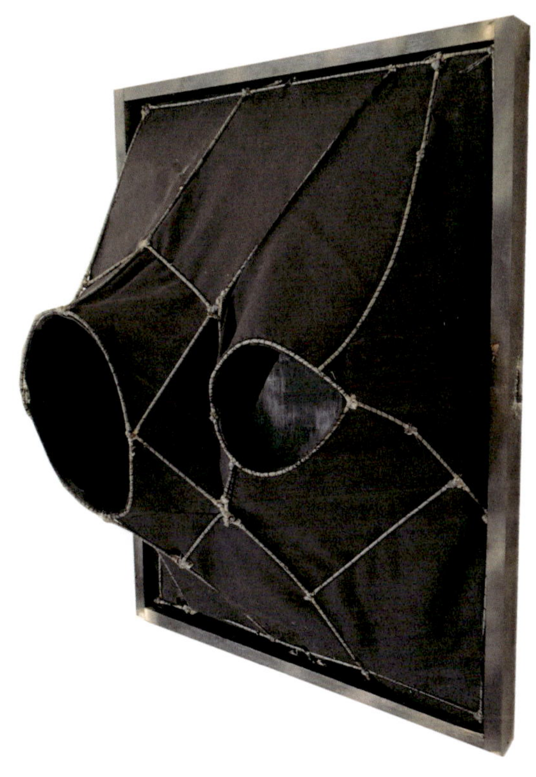

'Bontecaux'
Wire, cloth, thread, steel, in wood
panel, frame
30x20x16"
2020

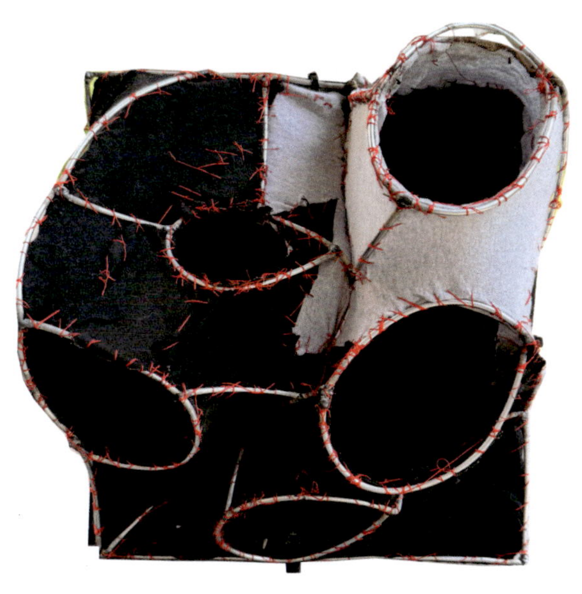

'Bontecaux #13'
Welded steel wire, cotton fabric,
thread, laquer, zip ties, on wood panel
9.25x9.5x4.5"
2024

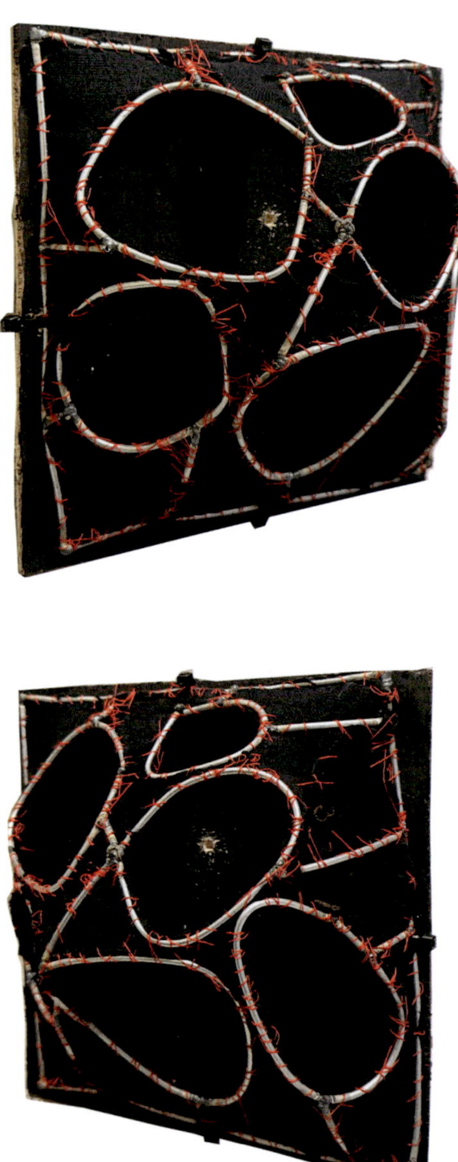

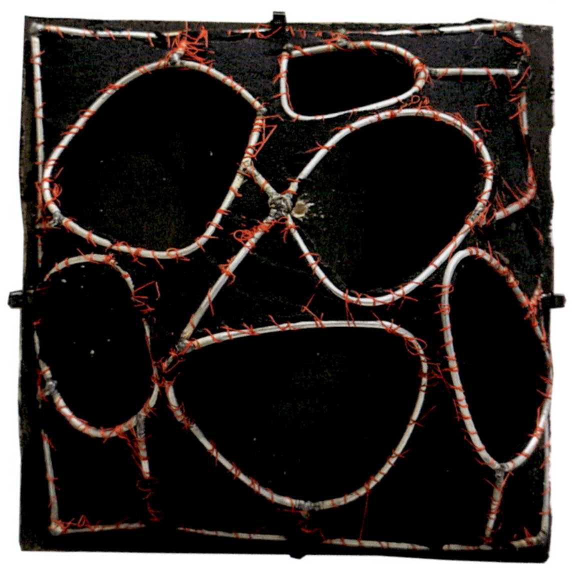

'Bontecaux #12'
Welded steel wire, cotton fabric,
thread, zip ties, on wood panel
8x8x3.5""
2024

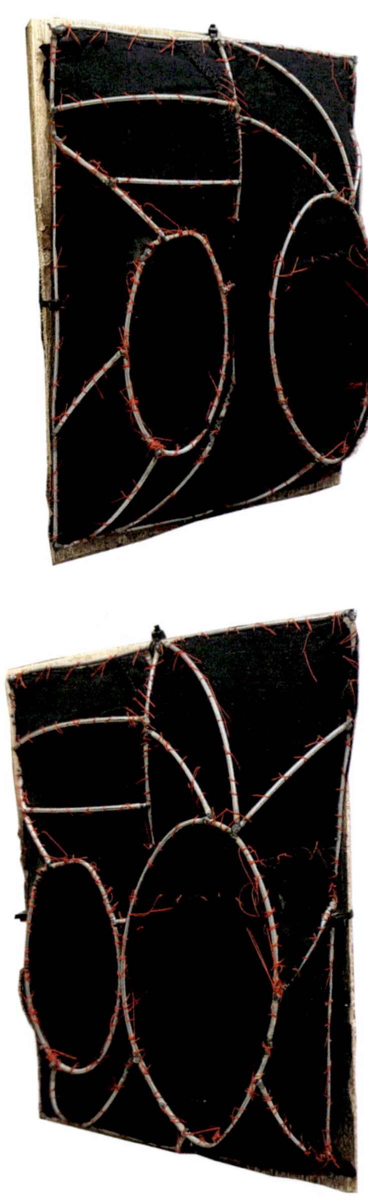

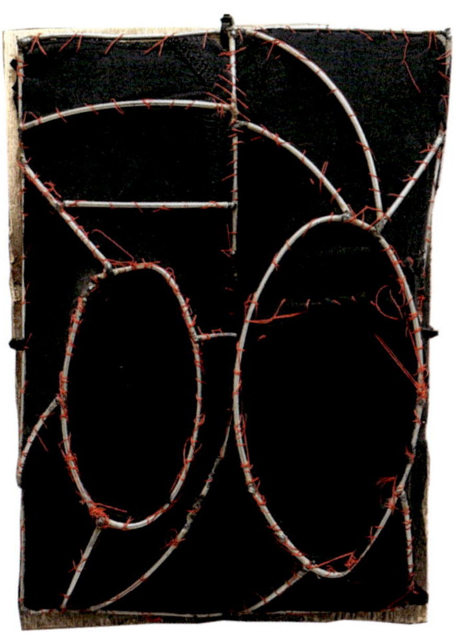

'Bontecaux #11'
Welded steel wire, cotton fabric,
thread, zip ties, on wood panel
11.75x8.5x2.75"
2024

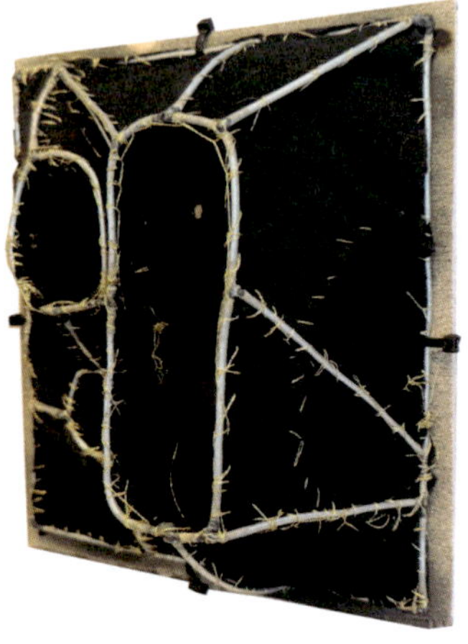

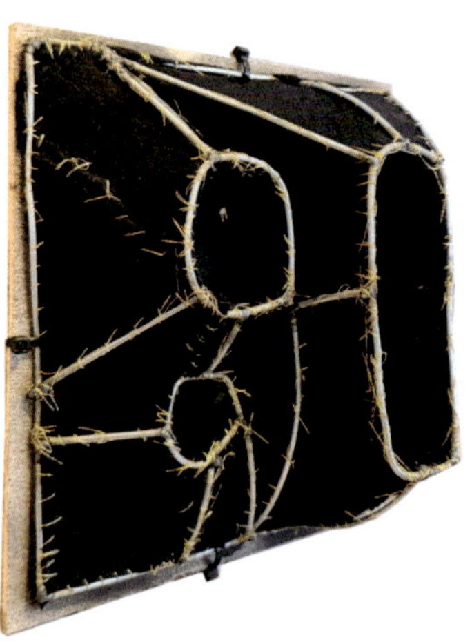

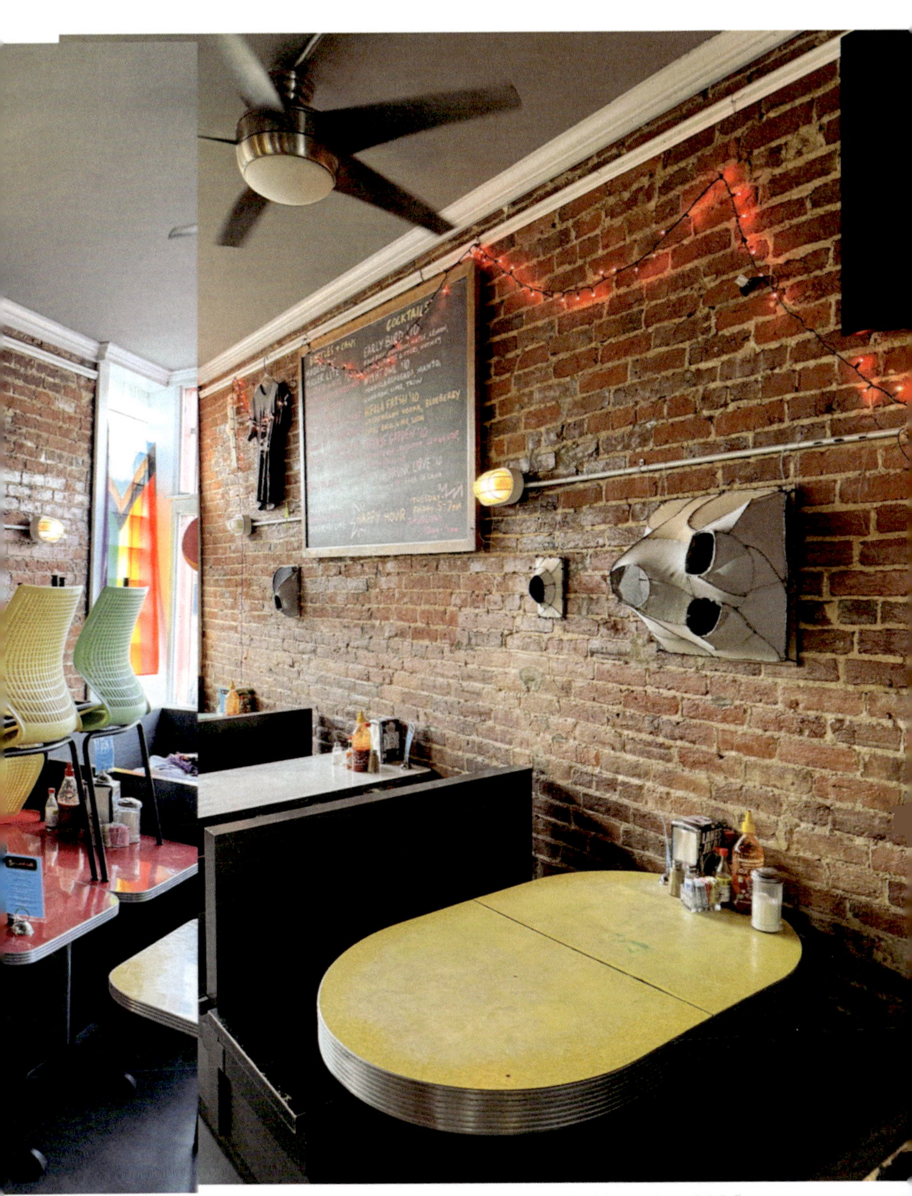

'installation at 821 Cafe in Richmond, VA, November 2024

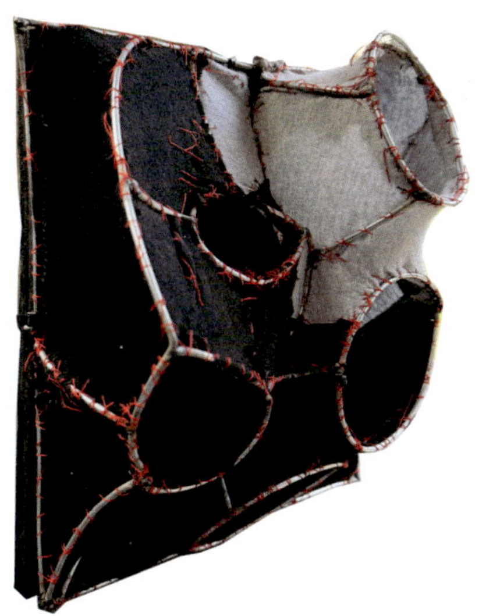

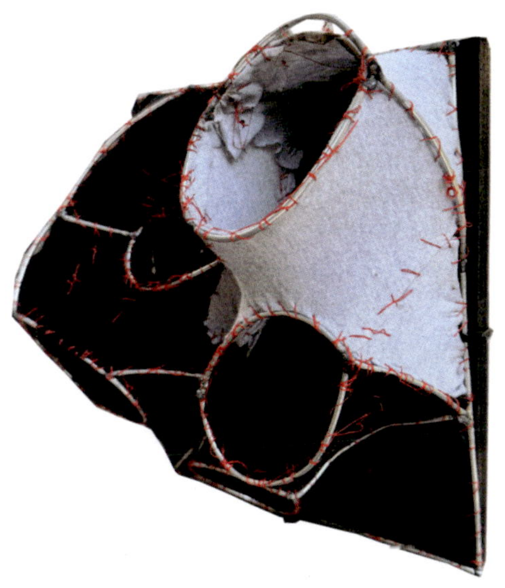